From Bystanders To Upstanders

A Teacher's Guide to Addressing and Preventing Bullying in Schools

Stuart W. Macmillan

Copyright © 2023 Stuart Macmillan

All rights reserved.

ISBN: 978-1-99-105626-9

DEDICATION

This book is dedicated to those that have the courage to follow through and create a safe and easy to follow procedure to deal with and prevent and eliminate bullying in schools.

INTRODUCTION

Bullying in any form should not be tolerated. All children have the right to be schooled in a safe environment. All schools have the obligation to ensure that the school is safe for all its pupils and staff.

This guide is presented for you to follow and set up easy to follow procedures so that all forms of bullying are easily handled and properly addressed. At no time should a student or staff member find themselves in a position in which they do not know where to turn for help.

This must be clearly defined and never should a person be turned away who is feeling threatened or scared.

BULLYING

Bullying has been a persistent issue in schools since schooling began and it is a major concern for students, teachers, and parents alike. Teachers have the responsibility to not only address bullying when it occurs but to also prevent it from happening in the first place. In order to do this, we must shift from being bystanders to upstanders.

The first step in addressing bullying is to create a safe and supportive environment in the classroom. This can be achieved by promoting positive relationships and respect among students, setting clear expectations for behaviour, and being proactive in addressing any instances of bullying when they occur. Teachers can also incorporate activities that promote kindness and empathy, such as group discussions or service projects, to create a positive school culture.

Another important step is to educate students on what bullying is and the harm it causes. This can be done through classroom lessons, workshops, and presentations. Students should also be made aware of the various forms of bullying, including physical, verbal, and cyberbullying. Additionally, teachers can provide resources for students who may be struggling with bullying, such as counselling services or support groups.

It is also crucial for teachers to provide training for themselves and other staff members on how to recognize and respond to bullying. This can include techniques for de-escalating conflicts, how to report incidents, and how to support victims. Regular assessments and evaluations of the school's anti-bullying policies can also help ensure that they are effective and properly implemented.

Finally, involving parents and the community in an effort to prevent bullying can also be extremely beneficial. This can include workshops, parent-teacher meetings, and community events that focus on promoting a positive school culture and addressing bullying.

It is up to everyone - teachers, students, parents, and the community - to work together to create a safe and supportive school environment where bullying is not tolerated. By shifting from being bystanders to upstanders and taking proactive steps to address and prevent bullying, we can help create a better future for all students.

THE BYSTANDER ROLE

The bystander role in bullying refers to the individuals who are present when bullying occurs, but are not directly involved as either the victim or the bully. Bystanders can have a significant impact on the situation and their actions (or lack thereof) can either escalate or de-escalate the bullying.

When bystanders take a passive approach and do not intervene, it sends a message to the bully that their behaviour is acceptable, and can lead to further bullying. In contrast, when bystanders actively intervene and support the victim, it sends a message to the bully that their behaviour is not tolerated, and can help to de-escalate the situation.

Additionally, the actions of bystanders can also impact the victim's emotional well-being. When bystanders offer support and assistance to the victim, it can help to reduce their feelings of isolation and increase their sense of safety. However, when bystanders remain passive and do not offer support, it can reinforce the victim's feelings of powerlessness and increase their distress.

WHAT IS THE BYSTANDER EFFECT

The bystander effect in bullying situations refers to the phenomenon where individuals are less likely to intervene or help a victim when they are in the presence of others. This can be a significant barrier in preventing bullying, as witnesses to bullying may not take action or report incidents.

To overcome this, it is important to empower students to become "upstanders" rather than bystanders. This means encouraging them to take action and stand up for others who are being bullied. Teachers can foster this by teaching students about the importance of empathy and compassion, and by providing them with the tools and skills they need to intervene safely and effectively in bullying situations.

In addition to teaching students, teachers can also set an example by actively promoting upstanding behaviour in their own classrooms. This includes modeling respectful behaviour and addressing bullying incidents in a prompt and effective manner. Teachers can also encourage students to report bullying and provide support for those who come forward.

Finally, it is important to create a school culture that supports and values upstanding behaviour. This can be achieved through school-wide initiatives, such as anti-bullying campaigns, and by rewarding and recognizing students who demonstrate upstanding behaviour. By creating a culture of empathy, respect, and inclusion, we can encourage students to be active participants in preventing bullying, and create a safer and more supportive environment for all.

In the end, we will remember not the words of our enemies but the silence of our friends.

Martin Luther King, Jr.

WHY SOME PEOPLE CHOOSE NOT TO INTERVENE

While many students are willing to stand up to bullies, others choose to remain silent and do nothing to intervene. There are several reasons why students may choose not to intervene in bullying situations, including fear of retaliation, a lack of confidence, and peer pressure.

Fear of retaliation is one of the main reasons students choose not to intervene in bullying situations. They are afraid that the bully will turn on them and become their next target. This fear can be particularly pronounced if the bully has a history of violence or if they have threatened the bystander in the past.

A lack of confidence can also prevent students from intervening in bullying situations. Some students may feel that they are not assertive enough to stand up to a bully and may worry about making the situation worse. Additionally, some students may not know what to do or say, or may not feel confident enough to take action.

Peer pressure is another reason why students may choose not to intervene in bullying situations. They may be worried about what their friends will think if they stand up to the bully or if they report the incident to an authority figure. They may also worry about losing their social standing or being ostracized by their peers.

To overcome these barriers, it is important to educate students about the importance of speaking out against bullying. Schools can create a supportive and safe environment by promoting respect, tolerance, and understanding. Additionally, schools can provide students with training on how to respond to bullying, how to report incidents, and how to provide support to the victim.

> There are no innocent bystanders.

William S. Burroughs

HOW TO SAFELY BECOME AN UPSTANDER

Bullying can have a devastating impact on students, affecting their mental and emotional health, and creating a hostile learning environment. As a result, it is important for students to feel empowered to intervene as an "upstander" when they see bullying taking place.

Here are some tips to help students safely and effectively intervene. You can use these in any class or situation. Sometimes you only have to keep these in mind so if you see some behaviour that could lead to bullying, you can start a conversation with students nearby but are within earshot of potential offenders.

Other ways are to take one topic per day and discuss it quickly before or after a class, sports event or class roll-call.

1. Speak up: If you see bullying happening, speak up and let the bully know that their behaviour is unacceptable. You can say something like, "That's not okay" or "Stop it." By speaking out, you can show the victim that they are not alone and that others are willing to stand up for them.

2. Report the incident: If you are unable to intervene safely or if the bullying continues, report the incident to a trusted adult, such as a teacher, counsellor, or school administrator. They can help to resolve the situation and ensure that the victim is safe.

3. Support the victim: Show support to the victim by sitting with them at lunch, including them in group activities, or simply being a friendly ear to listen. This can help the victim feel less isolated and more confident.

4. Be an ally: Stand up for those who are being bullied, even if they are not your close friends. By doing so, you can show the bully that their behaviour is not acceptable and that their actions have consequences.

5. Be proactive: Try to prevent bullying before it starts by promoting a culture of kindness and respect in your school. You can do this by participating in anti-bullying campaigns, volunteering for peer mentoring programs, or simply being a positive role model.

6. Seek help: If you are experiencing bullying yourself, seek help from a trusted adult. You can also reach out to friends, family members, or organizations for support and guidance.

USING TECHNOLOGY TO BE AN UPSTANDER

Here are some ways students can safely use technology to act as an upstander when they see bullying. You can discuss these with your students. Go through them one by one and ask for their input and create a list and then come to conclusions on each sub-topic.

These can be presented in discussions or used as a general handout for students. Keep copies of these on a file that students can download from your website, Google Drive account or internal network.

1. **Report incidents**: Many schools have online reporting systems that allow students to report bullying anonymously. This can be a safe and effective way to get help for the victim and hold the bully accountable for their actions. If your school does not have a reporting system, follow our guidelines below to set one up as soon as possible.

2. **Use social media for good**: Social media can be used to spread awareness about bullying and to show support for the victim. For example, students can share anti-bullying messages, post positive comments, or create campaigns to raise awareness about the issue. Do not fall into the trap of naming and shaming online or else you could create more problems.

3. **Document incidents**: If you witness bullying taking place online, take screenshots or save videos as evidence. This can be used to show administrators what is happening and to hold the bully accountable. Again this could be

formed into a school database supervised and monitored by staff.

4. **Get help**: If you are experiencing bullying online, reach out to a trusted adult, friend, or organisation for support. You can also use technology to access resources and information about bullying and how to get help. Talk to your parents and teacher!

5. **Promote kindness**: Use technology to promote a culture of kindness and respect online. This can include sharing positive messages, calling out cyber bullying when you see it, and being a supportive and empathetic friend to others.

Online Groups: As with point 5, you can create online groups connected to your school that promotes social positivity and caring between students and the community.

IMPLEMENTING THE BYSTANDERS TO UPSTANDERS IN BULLYING PREVENTION

Using the guides in this book, connect each section to different areas of school life and classes. Bullying is not a topic that will not go away and becoming an upstander and reporting all forms of bullying and violent behaviour should be discussed in every class to create an overall culture where bullying will not be tolerated.

Name-calling and the occasional outburst may be one-off incidents but as a teacher, you need to keep an eye on these types of actions and ensure they do not escalate or continue. Bullying is an ongoing behaviour, not an occasional thing. You just have to make sure these occasions don't increase by "nipping them in the bud".

Here are some outlines of how to develop the "no bullying" culture combined with the bystander and upstander strategy...

- Education: Provide education on the impact of bullying and how to be an upstander. Copy sections of this book and use them in handouts or class material.

- Encouragement: Encourage students to speak up and take action when they witness bullying. Emphasising the development of the principles of good character and values such as courage and empathy helps in this area.

- Modelling: Provide positive role models who demonstrate upstanding behaviour. Articles in the News are good to refer to in discussions where bystanders have spoken up to help arrest criminals.

- Create a safe environment: Ensure that students feel safe reporting bullying and that there are consequences for bullies. You must have a system in place for reporting bullying so that all students and parents know the procedures to follow.

- Collaboration: Collaborate with teachers, administrators, parents, and community organizations to address bullying. Everyone in your school needs to be a part of your policy for it to work.

- Reinforcement: Reinforce upstanding behaviour through positive reinforcement and rewards. Accentuating the positive is the best way to encourage upstanding behaviour and the non-tolerance of anti-social behaviour.

Each of these is covered in the following chapters.

EDUCATING STUDENTS ON THE IMPACT OF BULLYING AND HOW TO BE AN UPSTANDER

One of the most important areas to get the ball rolling is education, as discussed in the implementation section above. Let's take a look at some ways this can be done properly. Some of these tips overlap with other aspects but that is life - everything is interconnected.

Introduction

Bullying is a persistent issue that affects millions of students across the world. It causes harm to both the victims and witnesses of the bullying behaviour, making it a crucial problem to address.

In order to prevent bullying and promote positive behaviour, it is essential to educate students about the impact of bullying and empower them to become upstanders.

Upstanders are individuals who take a stand against bullying and actively work to create a safe and inclusive environment. By educating students about the impact of bullying, they can gain a deeper understanding of how their actions and words can affect others and learn how to be an upstander.

In this manual, we will provide steps and guidance for educating students about the impact of bullying and how to be an upstander.

Starting a Conversation

It is important to start an open and honest conversation with students about bullying and its impact. This can create a safe and inclusive environment where students feel comfortable discussing the topic.

To start a conversation:

- Encourage open and honest discussions about bullying and its impact.

- Create a safe and inclusive environment where students feel comfortable sharing their experiences and thoughts.

Providing Resources

Offering students resources such as books, videos, and websites that address bullying and its impact can help them understand the issue from different perspectives and develop a greater understanding of the topic.

To provide resources:

- Make a list of relevant books, videos, and websites on bullying and its impact.

- Encourage students to use these resources to gain a deeper understanding of the topic.

Engaging in Role-Play Activities

Engaging students in role-play activities that simulate bullying scenarios can allow students to experience the impact of bullying from different perspectives and learn how to respond in a positive way.

To engage in role-play activities:

- Plan and conduct role-play activities that simulate bullying scenarios.

- Encourage students to experience the impact of bullying from different perspectives.

- Teach students how to respond in a positive way.

Involving Students in Creating Solutions

Encouraging students to take an active role in creating solutions to bullying can help them understand the importance of their actions and empower them to create a positive and inclusive environment.

To involve students in creating solutions:

- Encourage students to take an active role in creating solutions to bullying.

- Help students understand the importance of their actions in creating a positive and inclusive environment.

- Empower students to take action and create solutions.

Reinforcing Positive Behavior

Reinforcing positive behaviour by recognising and rewarding students who act as upstanders can encourage students to continue to act in a positive and supportive manner.

To reinforce positive behaviour:

- Recognise and reward students who act as upstanders.

- Encourage students to continue to act in a positive and supportive manner.

- Promote positive behaviour and attitudes.

Summary

By educating students about the impact of bullying and empowering them to become upstanders, we can create a safer and more inclusive environment for all students. Teachers and educators have a unique opportunity to make a lasting impact on the lives of students and help them become responsible and compassionate individuals.

This manual provides steps and guidance for educating students about the impact of bullying and how to be an upstander. Use these steps to make a positive impact on the lives of your students and create a safer and more inclusive environment for all.

What hurts the victim most is not the cruelty of the oppressor, but the silence of the bystander.

Elie Wiesel

RESOURCES

You can find many resources that are helpful to reinforce the aspects of bystanding and upstanding as well as overall actions and reactions to anti-social behaviour. This list is just a brief guide collected from international sources but any online search will uncover more.

URL links are not supplied as these always change over time.

Books:

- "The Bully, the Bullied, and the Bystander" by Barbara Coloroso

- "Stick Up for Yourself!: Every Kid's Guide to Personal Power & Positive Self-Esteem" by Gershen Kaufman

- "The Learning Community: Lessons in Pursuit of Genius" by Michael Grinder

- "Words Wound: Delete Cyberbullying and Make Kindness Go Viral" by Justin W. Patchin and Sameer Hinduja

- "Odd Girl Out: The Hidden Culture of Aggression in Girls" by Rachel Simmons

Videos:

- "Bully" (2011) Documentary

- "The Making of a Bully" (2007) Documentary

- "Cyberbullying: How to Stop It" (2018) Educational Video

- "The Bystander Revolution" (2020) Educational Video

- "Stand Up to Bullying" (2021) Public Service Announcement

Websites:

- StopBullying.gov

- PACER's National Bullying Prevention Center

- The Bully Project

- The Cyberbullying Research Center

- Anti-Bullying Alliance (UK)

HOW TO PLAN AND CONDUCT ROLE-PLAY ACTIVITIES THAT SIMULATE BULLYING SCENARIOS

Role-play activities are a great way to make ideas sink in. Combining participation and observation helps students learn and remember anything. Plan them well to ensure the main message is included and that role-play does not overlap into actual behaviour.

1. Identify the purpose: Determine why you want to conduct role-play activities and what you hope to achieve.

2. Choose the scenario: Select a bullying scenario that you want to

simulate. This could be verbal, physical, or cyberbullying.

3. Prepare materials: Make sure you have everything you need for the activity, such as props or costumes. Soft objects are preferred to make sure no hard comes to anyone.

4. Assign roles: Decide who will play which role in the scenario and make sure each person is aware of what is expected of them. It is best to discuss things first to ensure that people who have been bullies or are emotionally affected by bullying are not put into a compromising position by being involved if they do not want to be.

5. Brief participants: Give a brief overview of the activity, including the scenario and the objectives. Explain what will happen during the role-play and what you expect from each participant. Ensure that participants use fictitious names and circumstances and that the use of actual physical abuse is to be pretended only and not involve full physical contact.

6. Conduct the activity: Allow the participants to act out the scenario, while being mindful to keep it respectful and safe.

7. Debrief: After the activity, lead a discussion with participants to reflect on what they learned, how they felt, and what they would do differently in real life.

8. Evaluate the activity: Assess the effectiveness of the role-play and make adjustments for future activities as needed.

9. Repeat: Conduct similar activities to reinforce the importance of bullying prevention and to give participants opportunities to apply what they learned.

On the following pages, you will find an example role-play for each of the three categories outlined above.

EXAMPLE OF ROLE-PLAY ACTIVITY 1

Scenario: *Cyberbullying on social media*

1. Purpose: To raise awareness about the dangers of cyberbullying and to give participants the opportunity to practice responding to it.

2. Choose the scenario: A student is being bullied on social media by a group of classmates, using hurtful comments and spreading false rumours.

3. Prepare materials: None needed, but participants may need access to a computer or Smartphone to simulate the scenario.

4. Assign roles: One person will play the victim, several others will play the cyber bullies, and others will play bystanders.

5. Brief participants: Explain that the role-play is designed to simulate a real-life situation of cyberbullying on social media. Emphasize the importance of respecting each

other during the activity and avoiding actual harm.

6. Conduct the activity: The victim is scrolling through their social media feed and sees the cyberbullying comments and rumours. The bystanders observe the situation and then decide how they will respond, either by intervening or ignoring it.

7. Debrief: After the role-play, lead a discussion to reflect on what was observed and experienced. Ask participants to share their thoughts and feelings about the situation. Discuss what could have been done differently to prevent or stop cyberbullying.

8. Evaluate the activity: Assess the effectiveness of the role-play in raising awareness about cyberbullying and the impact it can have.

9. Repeat: Repeat the activity or similar ones to reinforce the importance of bullying prevention and to give participants opportunities to practice responding to cyberbullying.

EXAMPLE OF ROLE-PLAY ACTIVITY 2

Scenario: *Verbal bullying in a school setting*

1. Purpose: To raise awareness about the impact of verbal bullying and to give participants the opportunity to practice responding to it.

2. Choose the scenario: A student is being bullied by a group of classmates, using verbal insults and name-calling.

3. Prepare materials: None needed.

4. Assign roles: One person will play the victim, several others will play the bullies, and others will play witnesses.

5. Brief participants: Explain that the role-play is designed to simulate a real-life situation of verbal bullying in a school setting. Emphasize the importance of respecting each other during the activity and avoiding actual physical or emotional harm.

6. Conduct the activity: The victim enters the scene and is immediately surrounded by the bullies who start to insult and name-call. The witnesses observe the situation and then decide how they will respond, either by intervening or ignoring it.

7. Debrief: After the role-play, lead a discussion to reflect on what was observed and experienced. Ask participants to share their thoughts and feelings about the situation. Discuss what could have been done differently to prevent or stop the bullying.

8. Evaluate the activity: Assess the effectiveness of the role-play in raising awareness about verbal bullying and the impact it can have.

9. Repeat: Repeat the activity or similar ones to reinforce the importance of bullying prevention and to give participants opportunities to practice responding to bullying.

EXAMPLE OF ROLE-PLAY ACTIVITY 3

Scenario: *Physical bullying in a playground setting*

1. Purpose: To raise awareness about the dangers of physical bullying and to give participants the opportunity to practice responding to it.

2. Choose the scenario: A student is being physically bullied by a group of classmates, using pushing and shoving.

3. Prepare materials: None needed.

4. Assign roles: One person will play the victim, several others will play the bullies, and others will play witnesses.

5. Brief participants: Explain that the role-play is designed to simulate a real-life situation of physical bullying in a playground setting. Emphasize the importance of respecting each other during the activity and avoiding actual physical harm.

6. Conduct the activity: The victim enters the scene and is immediately surrounded by the bullies who start to push and shove. The witnesses observe the situation and then decide how they will respond, either by intervening or ignoring it.

7. Debrief: After the role-play, lead a discussion to reflect on what was observed and experienced. Ask participants to share their thoughts and feelings about the situation. Discuss what could have been done differently to prevent or stop physical bullying.

8. Evaluate the activity: Assess the effectiveness of the role-play in raising awareness about physical bullying and the impact it can have.

9. Repeat: Repeat the activity or similar ones to reinforce the importance of bullying prevention and to give participants opportunities to practice responding to physical bullying.

HELP STUDENTS UNDERSTAND THE IMPORTANCE OF THEIR ACTIONS

You can help students understand the importance of their actions in creating a positive and inclusive environment by incorporating the following strategies. Some of these were touched on in the implementation section above but are repeated in other ways just in the way they should be repeated in real life to ensure the points are driven home and remembered.

- Model positive behaviour: The teacher can model positive behaviour, treating all students with respect and kindness.

- Emphasize the impact of actions: The teacher can help students understand the impact of their actions by explaining how words and actions can affect others.

- Use real-life examples: The teacher can use real-life examples to demonstrate the importance of creating a positive and inclusive environment, such as by sharing news stories or personal experiences.

- Encourage open communication: The teacher can foster open communication by creating a safe and supportive classroom environment where students can discuss their feelings and experiences.

- Promote teamwork and collaboration: The teacher can promote teamwork and collaboration by assigning group projects and activities that encourage students to work together and build relationships.

- Reinforce positive behaviour: The teacher can reinforce positive behaviour by recognizing and praising students for their efforts to create a positive and inclusive environment.

- Address negative behaviour: The teacher can address negative behaviour by addressing it directly and explaining why it is not acceptable.

- Provide opportunities for reflection: The teacher can provide opportunities for reflection by asking students to think about their actions and the impact they have on others.

By using these strategies, you can help students understand the importance of their actions in creating a positive and inclusive environment, and encourage them to make a positive impact on their peers and community.

MORE WAYS FOR YOU TO HELP STUDENTS

If they come to you and ask, "How do I be an Upstander when the bullies and bigger and tougher than I am?"

Here are some things you can tell them to help them be more confident:

- Seek support from a trusted adult: This can be a parent, teacher, counsellor, or another authority figure that can help you address the situation and provide guidance.

- Stand up for yourself confidently: Confronting bullies and showing that you are not afraid can sometimes be enough to make them stop.

- Use humour: Humour can diffuse a tense situation and take the wind out of a bully's sails.

- Avoid physical confrontation: If the bully is physically stronger, it's best to avoid physical confrontations and instead seek help from someone in authority.

- Practice assertiveness: Learning how to assert yourself in a calm and confident manner can help you handle confrontations with bullies more effectively.

- Build a support network: Surrounding yourself with friends who will support you can give you strength and help you feel less alone.

MORE STRATEGIES THAT YOUR SCHOOL CAN IMPLEMENT TO REDUCE BULLYING

This is not an exhaustive list but there are many ways that every school should implement to ensure the elimination of bullying.

On the pages following these points, you will find out how to implement each strategy.

- Anti-bullying policies and procedures
- Teacher and staff training
- Student education and awareness programs

- Anonymous reporting systems
- Support and counselling services for victims and bullies
- Parental involvement and education
- Collaboration with community organizations
- Monitoring and intervention strategies
- Positive behaviour reinforcement
- Consequences for bullies.

ANTI-BULLYING POLICIES AND PROCEDURES

1. Conduct a review of current policies and practices to identify gaps or areas for improvement.

2. Involve relevant stakeholders, such as students, parents, teachers, and administrators, in policy development.

3. Define clear and specific definitions of bullying behaviour.

4. Outline steps for reporting and investigating bullying incidents.

5. Establish a system for recording and tracking bullying incidents.

6. Provide clear consequences for bullies.

7. Foster a positive school culture that emphasizes respect and inclusion.

8. Ensure that all staff are trained on the policies and procedures.

9. Regularly review and evaluate the effectiveness of the policies and procedures.

10. Encourage open communication and collaboration between students, parents, and staff.

Anti-bullying policies and procedures aim to prevent and address bullying behaviour in schools and workplace settings. Here are some key steps to developing effective anti-bullying policies:

1. Define Bullying: Clearly define what constitutes as bullying, including physical, verbal, sexual harassment, and cyberbullying. This definition should be included

in the policy and made available to everyone in your schools.

2. Involve Stakeholders: Involve relevant stakeholders in the development process, including students, parents, teachers, and staff. This can ensure that all perspectives are taken into account and that the policy is well-received by everyone.

3. Establish Reporting Procedures: Clearly establish reporting procedures for individuals who experience or witness bullying. This can include a reporting hotline, forms at the school office that are easily accessible, designating a person to receive reports, and an online reporting form.

4. Provide Training: Provide training for students, teachers, and staff on how to recognise and prevent bullying, as well as how to respond appropriately to reports of bullying. Keeping these procedures on your website is a good way to ensure everyone knows at all times.

5. Implement Consequences: Establish clear consequences for

those who engage in bullying behaviour. These consequences should be age-appropriate, in line with the law and should be consistently enforced.

6. Monitor and Evaluate: Regularly monitor and evaluate the effectiveness of the policy and make changes as necessary. This can include conducting surveys, gathering feedback, and analyzing data on bullying incidents.

7. Foster a Positive Culture: Encourage a positive school and workplace culture that values respect, kindness, empathy and inclusivity. This can help prevent bullying behaviour from occurring in the first place and create a supportive environment for those who may have experienced bullying.

By following these steps, schools can develop comprehensive and effective anti-bullying policies and procedures that can help prevent and address bullying behaviour. Additionally, by fostering a positive culture and providing support to those who have experienced bullying, schools can create a safe and inclusive environment for all.

This refers to staff and teachers as well. If there is a bullying culture between staff, this is an extremely bad example for students. It must be taken seriously and procedures for handling staff bullying must also be included.

DEFINING BULLYING

Bullying can be defined as repetitive, intentional behaviour that is intended to harm or intimidate another person. This can take many forms, including physical, verbal, or cyberbullying. A clear definition of bullying should include the following elements:

1. Repetitive behaviour: Bullying involves repeated actions or incidents, rather than a one-time occurrence.

2. Intentional actions: Bullying is a deliberate act, not an accidental

one. The action is intended to harm or intimidate the target.

3. Harm or intimidation: This causes harm or fear in the target person, and can include physical, psychological, or emotional harm.

It is also important to note that bullying can occur between individuals of any age, and in any setting, and can be motivated by factors such as race, religion, gender, or sexual orientation. By clearly defining bullying, organizations can establish a common understanding of the issue and take steps to prevent and address it effectively.

HOW TO INVOLVE STAKEHOLDERS

Having a solid and effective policy is important in creating a safe and respectful environment. That's why involving a diverse range of stakeholders is key. Let's go over the reasons why this is important:

- Awareness and buy-in: Inviting stakeholders to be part of the process helps raise awareness about bullying and can increase their support for the policy.

- Diverse perspectives: Including stakeholders from different backgrounds and perspectives can ensure that all viewpoints are considered and that the policy is well-received.

- Improved policy: Stakeholders can provide valuable insights and suggestions for making the policy even better, such as identifying high-risk areas for bullying or suggesting specific consequences for bullies.

- Implementation support: By having stakeholders involved in the process, organizations can build support for putting the policy into action, which can lead to more effective results.

- Increased accountability: When stakeholders are a part of the process, they are more likely to hold themselves and others accountable for following the policy, which can increase its effectiveness.

Involving stakeholders in developing an anti-bullying policy is a win-win situation. It leads to a comprehensive and effective policy that has increased support for implementation. So let's work together to create a safe and respectful environment for everyone!

EXAMPLE OF A SCHOOL ANTI-BULLYING POLICY

Here is an example of how your policy can be set up. You should first involve all stakeholders in the creation of this policy and once complete, all parents and students have access to this policy, perhaps on your school website.

If you need help with this, you can contact Interweb Education for personal assistance. We provide professional systems analysis and project management staff to guide you through or manage it as a project on your behalf as an offsite consultant. If you need assistance with a website, Interweb Apps offers a wide range of online services

(See the end of this book for contact information).

The example policy starts on the following page. This is just a brief outline and must be expanded upon to reflect the culture and values of your school and its community.

Our Schools Anti-Bullying Bullying Policy

Purpose:

1. This policy is designed to promote a safe and respectful learning environment free from bullying and harassment. The school is committed to providing a safe and secure environment for all students, employees and visitors and will not tolerate bullying behaviour.

Definition of Bullying:

2. Bullying is defined as repeated, intentional behaviour that is intended to harm or intimidate another person. This can include physical, verbal, or emotional abuse, cyberbullying, and harassment.

Reporting:

3. Any individual who witnesses or experiences bullying is encouraged to report it to a teacher, counsellor, or other school staff member. Reports can also be made anonymously, but the school encourages individuals to provide their names to assist in the investigation and resolution of the incident.

Investigation and Resolution:

4. The school will thoroughly investigate all reported incidents of bullying and take appropriate action to resolve the situation. This may include disciplinary action for the individual(s) involved, support for the victim, and education for all students on the harm caused by bullying behaviour.

Prevention and Education:

5. The school will provide education and training to students, staff, and parents on bullying prevention and how to respond to bullying incidents. This education will be ongoing and will include topics such as recognizing bullying behaviour, bystander intervention, and the importance of reporting bullying.

Confidentiality:

6. The school will maintain confidentiality to the greatest extent possible during an investigation. Information will be shared only with those individuals who have a need to know in order to ensure a thorough investigation and resolution.

Disciplinary Action:

7. Individuals who engage in bullying may face disciplinary action up to and including suspension or expulsion. The school may also involve law enforcement if the bullying behaviour constitutes a criminal act.

Review:

8. This policy will be reviewed and updated annually to ensure it remains effective in promoting a safe and respectful learning environment.

ESTABLISHING REPORTING PROCEDURES

Establishing clear and effective reporting procedures for bullying in a school is important to ensure that incidents are promptly addressed and resolved. Here are the steps to consider when setting up reporting procedures:

1. Encourage reporting: Create a safe and supportive environment where students, teachers, and staff feel comfortable reporting incidents of bullying. Provide multiple reporting options, such as a confidential reporting system, a designated

reporting person, or an online reporting form.

2. Establish a clear process: Clearly outline the steps that will be taken after a report is made, including who will be notified and how incidents will be investigated. This can help ensure that incidents are handled consistently and effectively.

3. Train staff: Provide training for teachers and staff on how to recognize, respond to, and report incidents of bullying. Ensure that they understand the importance of taking prompt action to address bullying and know how to follow the reporting procedures.

4. Communicate with students and families: Make sure that students and families understand the reporting procedures and the importance of reporting incidents of bullying. Encourage students to speak up and provide support for those who come forward.

5. Document and track incidents: Keep accurate records of all incidents of bullying, including who was involved, when and where the incident occurred, and the outcome. This information can be used to identify patterns and trends and to help prevent future incidents.

By establishing clear and effective reporting procedures, schools can ensure that incidents of bullying are promptly addressed and resolved, creating a safer and more respectful learning environment for all students.

EXAMPLES OF REPORTING PROCEDURES

Here are some examples of reporting procedures for bullying in schools:

1. Confidential reporting system: Schools can provide students with a confidential reporting system, such as a hotline or an online form, where they can report incidents of bullying anonymously. This option can be particularly useful for students who are afraid of retaliation from the bully.

2. Designated reporting person: Schools can appoint a designated

person, such as a teacher, counsellor, or administrator, to receive and investigate reports of bullying. This person can provide support and guidance to students and ensure that incidents are addressed promptly.

3. Online reporting form: Schools can create an online reporting form that students, teachers, and staff can access to report incidents of bullying. This option can be convenient and easily accessible for those who want to report bullying but may not feel comfortable talking to someone face-to-face.

4. Anonymous tip line: Schools can set up an anonymous tip line where students and others can leave a message about incidents of bullying. This option can be particularly useful for students who are afraid to report incidents directly.

5. Reporting to teachers: Students can be encouraged to report incidents of bullying directly to their teachers. Teachers can then

follow established reporting procedures to ensure that incidents are addressed promptly and effectively.

By offering multiple reporting options and providing clear guidance on the reporting process, schools can create a safe and supportive environment where bullying is not tolerated and incidents are promptly addressed.

Even a small token such as leaving pieces of paper around in places at school can be a help:

I have received a nasty text or email
The phone number was:
....
Or, the email address was:
....
The message read:
....
....
....
(Hand this form into the school office)

DEVELOPING CONSEQUENCES

Here are some consequences for individuals who engage in bullying:

1. Disciplinary action: Schools can take disciplinary action against students who engage in bullying behaviour, such as suspension, detention, or loss of privileges.

2. Restorative justice: Schools can use restorative justice programs to address bullying. These programs

bring the perpetrator and victim together to discuss the impact of the actions and come up with a plan to repair the harm done.

3. Counselling and support: Students who engage in bullying can be required to attend counselling or receive other support services to address the underlying issues that may contribute to their behaviour.

4. Education and awareness: Schools can require students who engage in bullying behaviour to participate in education and awareness programs designed to help them understand the impact of their actions and how to change their behaviour.

5. Parent involvement: Schools can involve parents in addressing bullying behaviour by informing them of incidents and requiring them to participate in efforts to change their child's behaviour.

By implementing consequences for bullying behaviour, schools can send a clear message that bullying will not be tolerated and can help prevent future incidents.

Always ensure all punishments or actions are covered by your local laws.

MONITORING AND EVALUATING YOUR PROCEDURES

Monitoring and evaluating bullying in schools is crucial for ensuring that incidents are being addressed effectively and for making any necessary adjustments to anti-bullying policies and procedures. Here are some steps that schools can take to monitor and evaluate bullying:

1. Regularly collect data: Schools can collect data on incidents of bullying through a variety of means, such as anonymous reporting systems, surveys, and observation. This data can be used to track trends,

identify areas of concern, and measure the effectiveness of anti-bullying efforts. This information can also provide insight into the types of bullying that are occurring and where they are taking place, allowing schools to tailor their anti-bullying efforts to specific areas of need.

2. Use a data analysis tool: Schools can use a data analysis tool, such as a spreadsheet or dashboard, to organize and analyze data on bullying incidents. This tool can help schools identify patterns, track trends, and measure the impact of anti-bullying efforts over time. Having access to this information can help schools make informed decisions about how to allocate resources and prioritize efforts to prevent bullying.

3. Involve stakeholders: Schools can involve stakeholders, such as students, teachers, staff, parents, and community members, in the monitoring and evaluation process.

This can help ensure that all perspectives are considered and that anti-bullying efforts are meeting the needs of the school community. Stakeholder input can also provide valuable feedback on the effectiveness of current efforts and ideas for how to improve them.

4. Conduct surveys: Schools can conduct regular surveys to gather feedback from students, teachers, and staff on their experiences with bullying and the effectiveness of anti-bullying efforts. This can help schools understand the impact of bullying on different groups within the school community and assess the effectiveness of anti-bullying initiatives.

5. Review policies and procedures: Schools should regularly review their anti-bullying policies and procedures to ensure that they are effective and up-to-date. This can involve seeking feedback from stakeholders, examining data on

incidents of bullying, and making any necessary adjustments to the policies and procedures. It is important to ensure that the policies and procedures are comprehensive, well-communicated, and consistently enforced to effectively address bullying in schools.

By regularly monitoring and evaluating bullying, schools can ensure that they are taking a comprehensive and effective approach to address this important issue. This can help create a safe and respectful school environment for all students and help prevent bullying from taking place.

If you need help setting up any of these procedures, we have qualified systems analysts and virtual assistants to help you with online forms, flowcharts, surveys and database design. See the end of this book for details.

YOUR SCHOOL'S POSITIVE CULTURE

Much in the same way as developing a values system for your school, your school must also adopt a policy that fosters a safe and friendly but disciplined culture.

Fostering a positive culture in schools is essential for creating a safe and supportive environment for students and staff. A positive school culture promotes academic achievement, reduces incidents of bullying, and fosters a sense of belonging for everyone in the school community.

Not only that but it helps children grow into people of good character and therefore helps them in their choice of career after leaving your care.

On the next page, we will go over some steps that you can implement in your school.

Steps that schools can take to foster a positive culture:

1. Encourage positive relationships: Schools can encourage positive relationships by promoting positive aspects of a person's character, such as kindness, respect, responsibility and empathy, and by addressing negative actions, such as bullying, anti-social and bad behaviour when they occur. This can include promoting positive interactions between students and staff, creating opportunities for students to work together, and promoting peer-to-peer mentorship programs.

2. Involve students in decision-making: Schools can involve students in decision-making by providing opportunities for student input and feedback, such as student councils and suggestion boxes. This not only gives students a voice in shaping their school experience but also empowers them to take ownership of their education and the school community.

3. Celebrate achievements and successes: Schools can celebrate achievements and successes by recognizing student and staff accomplishments, such as academic awards and good deeds, through special events and ceremonies. This can help create a positive and supportive school environment, as well as encourage students to set high goals and strive for excellence.

4. Encourage positive communication: Schools can encourage positive communication by promoting open

and respectful dialogue among students, staff, and parents. This can include opportunities for peer-to-peer and adult-to-student mentorship and counselling. Positive communication fosters understanding, trust, and collaboration among school community members, leading to a more supportive and inclusive environment.

5. Provide opportunities for student leadership: Schools can provide opportunities for student leadership by offering leadership training and opportunities for students to take on leadership roles, such as peer mentors and student ambassadors. These opportunities help students develop important skills, such as communication, teamwork, and problem-solving, while also providing them with a sense of purpose and meaning.

6. Foster a sense of community: Schools can foster a sense of

community by encouraging students, staff, and parents to participate in school-wide events, such as community service projects and cultural celebrations. These events help create a sense of belonging for everyone in the school community, fostering a positive and supportive school culture.

7. Promote positive values and beliefs: Schools can promote positive values and beliefs by incorporating them into the curriculum, extracurricular activities, and school-wide initiatives. This can include promoting values such as kindness, respect, inclusiveness, and responsibility, which are essential for building a positive school culture.

8. Encourage positive feedback: Schools can encourage positive feedback by promoting a culture of recognition and appreciation. This can include regular opportunities

for students and staff to give and receive positive feedback, such as through student-teacher conferences and staff appreciation events.

By fostering a positive culture, schools can create a safe and supportive environment for students and staff, where everyone feels valued and respected. This can lead to improved academic performance, higher levels of engagement and motivation, and a greater sense of belonging for everyone in the school community.

BECOMING A SCHOOL THAT IS AN UPSTANDER

Wrapping up all these processes and strategies mentioned in this manual, the best way for your school to show its commitment to preventing bullying is to enshrine your code into your overall school policy.

On the next page is a suggestion for outlining this policy or statement of commitment. Feel free to copy this and make any alteration you like to personalise it.

OUR PLEDGE AGAINST BULLYING

As a school community, we stand united in our commitment to creating a safe, inclusive and respectful environment for all students. We believe that every individual has the right to be treated with dignity and kindness, and it is our collective responsibility to stand up against any form of bullying.

Bullying has no place in our school, and it is our duty to ensure that every student feels safe and supported while they learn and grow. By acting as upstanders, we can work together to prevent and address bullying, and promote a positive school culture.

We all have a role to play in promoting kindness and understanding, and in speaking out against bullying whenever and wherever we see it happening. Whether it's standing up for someone who is being teased or excluded, or simply being a friend to someone who is feeling down, each and every one of us can make a difference.

We also recognise the importance of education and awareness in preventing bullying. This is why we will continue to provide resources and support to students, staff, and families so that we can work together to build a culture of respect and understanding.

Let us all take an active role in speaking out, supporting those who have been affected and promoting kindness and understanding. Together, we can make our school a place where everyone feels valued and supported. We are committed to creating a safe and inclusive school community where every student has the opportunity to reach their full potential.

I learned that courage was not the absence of fear, but the triumph over it. The brave man is not he who does not feel afraid, but he who conquers that fear.

Nelson Mandela.

STAFF TRAINING

Training and teaching staff in bullying reporting and handling procedures is critical for ensuring that all incidents of bullying are properly addressed and resolved in a timely manner. Here are some steps that schools can take to train teaching staff:

1. Clearly define bullying: As outlined before, you should have involved everyone in developing your definitions before training begins. These definitions must be part of the school's policies and should be shared with all staff members and

should be used consistently across the school.

2. Provide information on reporting procedures: Staff members should be trained on the proper reporting procedures for incidents of bullying. This should include how to identify incidents, who to report them to, and what information is needed to be provided in the report.

3. Discuss the consequences of bullying: Staff members should be informed about the consequences of bullying for the individual students involved, as well as for the school community as a whole. This can help to raise awareness about the seriousness of bullying and encourage staff members to take a proactive approach to prevent it.

4. Provide role-playing scenarios: Role-playing scenarios can be a helpful way to train staff members

on how to handle incidents of bullying. These scenarios can help staff members to understand how to respond appropriately in real-life situations and develop the necessary skills to handle bullying effectively.

5. Offer ongoing training and support: Schools should offer ongoing training and support to staff members to ensure that they are confident in their ability to handle bullying incidents. This can include regular refresher courses and ongoing support from a designated person in the school.

6. Foster open communication: Schools should foster open communication between staff members and students to help prevent incidents of bullying. Staff members should be encouraged to talk with students about bullying and to report any incidents that they observe.

7. Emphasise the importance of taking bullying seriously: Staff members should be reminded of the serious nature of bullying and of the need to take all incidents seriously. This can help to create a culture in which bullying is not tolerated and where staff members are vigilant in their efforts to prevent it.

8. Provide resources and support: Schools should provide resources and support to staff members to help them handle bullying incidents effectively. This can include access to counselling services, guidance on how to handle difficult situations, and access to resources and training materials.

By providing staff members with the training and support they need, schools can ensure that all bullying incidents are properly reported and handled. This can help to create a safe and supportive environment for students and staff and to prevent bullying from becoming a persistent problem in the school community.

SIGNS CHILDREN ARE BEING BULLIED

You will not always be told when bullying happens. You will need to keep an eye out for signs that something could be happening. Some signs that a child may be being bullied at school include:

- Unexplainable injuries

- Torn or damaged clothing

- Lost or destroyed belongings

- Frequent headaches or stomach aches

- Difficulty sleeping

- Changes in eating habits

- Declining grades

- Loss of interest in activities

- Avoidance of social situations

- Sudden mood changes or feelings of sadness, anger, or frustration

To identify these signs without interfering in their life, parents can communicate openly with their children and offer a safe, supportive environment for them to talk about their experiences. Additionally, parents can observe changes in their child's behaviour and listen to their concerns. Regular check-ins and being present for them can help them feel comfortable discussing any issues they may be facing at school.

See the end of this book for a link to download an eBook for FREE to help your students.

IF BULLYING IS REPORTED BY A THIRD PARTY

The best way for a teacher to handle bullying that they have been told about by another student is to...

1. Take the report seriously and provide support to the student who reported the bullying.

2. Privately talk to the student who is alleged to be bullying to gather more information and get their perspective.

3. Document the incident and any steps taken in response.

4. Inform the appropriate school officials, if necessary.

5. Take appropriate action to address the bullying, which may include creating a behaviour plan, involving the parents of both students, or referring the students for counselling.

6. Monitor the situation to ensure that the bullying has stopped.

It is important for the teacher to maintain confidentiality, but also to communicate with the necessary parties to effectively address the situation and promote a safe and positive learning environment for all students.

FAMILY BACKGROUNDS

Here are a few reasons why some kids engage in bullying behaviour with the support of their parents:

- Lack of awareness: Some parents may not be aware that their child's actions are seen as bullying and may not understand the harm it causes to the victims.

- Lack of involvement: Some parents may not be actively involved in their child's life and may not be aware of their behaviour at school or with their peers.

- Lack of understanding about bullying: Some parents may not fully understand what constitutes bullying or how to address it in a constructive and effective manner.

- Permissive parenting style: Some parents may have a permissive parenting style where they do not set clear rules and consequences for their child's behaviour, leading to the child feeling that their actions have no consequences.

- Family values and beliefs: Some parents may have values or beliefs that support aggressive or dominant behaviour, leading them to encourage or excuse their child's bullying behaviour.

- Personal experiences: Some parents may have been bullies themselves and may not understand the impact it has on others.

- Anti-Social Family Environment: The bully's home may be conducive to developing anti-social behaviour. The parent or family may be habitual protestors, criminals, alcoholics or drug addicts.

It is important to note that bullying is never acceptable and has serious consequences for both the victim and the perpetrator. Parents play a crucial role in preventing bullying and promoting respectful behaviour.

TIPS TO SEND HOME TO PARENTS

Send these tips on the next page home to your parents and post them on your school website or app in the parent section to help them. (If you don't have this type of access you can see some cost-effective solutions at interwebapps.biz).

Parent tips on Bullying

There are several ways you can do this and the best is through preparedness and communication so your child knows what to do and that a channel of dialogue is always open between you and your child/children. Here are a few tips I can think of that are part of our bullying elimination kits for schools:

1. Teach children how to handle bullying, including assertiveness and how to seek help.

2. Teach your kids about the definition of bullying: Constant harassment rather than a one-off time of name-calling.

3. Encourage open communication with your child about their experiences in school.

4. Foster your child's self-esteem and confidence through positive reinforcement.

5. Support anti-bullying policies and programs in the school.

6. Stay informed and communicate with the school about any bullying incidents.

7. Teach children to stand up for themselves and others in a respectful manner.

8. Encourage your child to engage in activities outside of school to build a support network.

WORKPLACE BULLYING

Your school, as with any other business, must have procedures to follow if bullying is happening between staff or teachers. You can find guidelines for this on most government websites to suit the country your school is based in. Here are a few tips though so you can keep an eye on the behaviour at your school and ensure all people are treated with kindness and have access to help.

Types of workplace bullying

- Verbal abuse or insults
- Isolation or exclusion

- Unfair treatment or criticism
- Intimidation or threats
- Overbearing supervision or micro-management
- Unjustified blame or fault-finding
- Unreasonable work demands or deadlines
- Tampering with work or property
- Spreading false information or rumours
- Physical aggression or intimidation.

What are some signs that your workmates or partners are experiencing workplace bullying?

- Stress and anxiety
- Low morale and job satisfaction
- Increased absenteeism or turnover
- Physical symptoms such as headaches or stomach problems

- Changes in sleep or eating habits
- Decreased work performance or productivity
- Avoidance of certain co-workers or situations
- Loss of confidence or self-esteem
- Feelings of helplessness or hopelessness.

How can one stop this behaviour or get out of that situation without damaging their career?

- Document incidents and their impact
- Communicate assertively and directly with the bully
- Seek support from colleagues, HR, or a union
- Create a safety plan
- Consider seeking outside help, such as counselling

- Consider a formal complaint or legal action as a last resort.

OTHER SERVICES TO ASSIST YOUR SCHOOL IN REDUCING BULLYING

Interweb Education

Provides personal assistance for

- Professional systems analysis and project management staff to guide you through setting up bullying policies and procedures and manage it as a project on your behalf as an offsite consultant.

- Virtual Assistants: To assist with regular administration tasks.

Website: https://interwebed.com

Email: admin@interwebed.com

Interweb Apps

If you need assistance with a website, Interweb Apps offers a wide range of online services and virtual assistants.

Website: https://interwebapps.biz

Email: admin@interwebapps.biz

To help your student more, here is a link to download our eBook, *Freedom From Being Bullied*. You can copy this eBook and give it to anyone you like.

Copy and paste this link into your browser to download the eBook from our online storage at Mega:

https://mega.nz/file/y9QgTD7K#eKP3KNHgTPkFD0LNQMVXzo64ez1FMcUV5INhjcNnkDI

www.ingramcontent.com/pod-product-compliance
Lightning Source LLC
Chambersburg PA
CBHW060332050426
42449CB00011B/2731